SAM SANTAMARIA

Sailor Moon

Life Events - Comic to Sinister

Stories • Poems • Photos

AuthorHouse™
1663 Liberty Drive
Bloomington, IN 47403
www.authorhouse.com
Phone: 1 (800) 839-8640

© 2019 Sam Santamaria. All rights reserved.

No part of this book may be reproduced, stored in a retrieval system, or transmitted
by any means without the written permission of the author.

Published by AuthorHouse 10/09/2019

ISBN: 978-1-7283-2106-6 (sc)
ISBN: 978-1-7283-2105-9 (e)

Library of Congress Control Number: 2019910692

Print information available on the last page.

Any people depicted in stock imagery provided by Getty Images are models,
and such images are being used for illustrative purposes only.
Certain stock imagery © Getty Images.

This book is printed on acid-free paper.

Because of the dynamic nature of the Internet, any web addresses or links contained in this book may have changed
since publication and may no longer be valid. The views expressed in this work are solely those of the author and do not
necessarily reflect the views of the publisher, and the publisher hereby disclaims any responsibility for them.

authorHOUSE

SAILOR MOON
Life Events - Comic to Sinister

* Stories * Poems * Photos by Sam Santamaria

July 2019, Hudson, Florida

for Sandy, Adrienne, Annika, Ian

my gratitude to Joy Buensalido, a good friend.

Contents

vii Acknowledgments

1 Introduction

3 Sailor Moon

7 The Blind Poet

9 Transitions

11 Seeing Red

17 Life in Outer Space

21 Fall Haiku

23 High Art, Low Art in NYC

29 Dreams

33 Daughter, Why the Furrowed Brow on a Pristine Morning?

35 Incident at the Shed

41 Jersey Diary

43 12 Zones

49 A Comic Odyssey Manila-Philadelphia-New York-New Jersey

59 Twin Towers

67 Rigoberto, Mirrored

69 He's Not Meh

71 Food – Some Mysteries and Memories

Acknowledgments

This book took shape in printed form with the persistent encouragement and hopeful motivation – from start to end, of my wife, Sandy. On my birthday in 2018, she gave me the tablet on which I strung together my decades worth of thoughts into the poems and stories of Sailor Moon. She also took the photo on the back cover, as I read the graphic novel of my son, Ian. Mrs. Sevilla, my grade school teacher told me to stay after class and write paragraphs, feeling confident that the exercise would bear a fruitful outcome in the future beyond her years. My publisher's check-in coordinator, Mark Francis never gave up until my complete manuscript hurdled all the text evaluator's initial stringent requirements for publication. And my dear mother, Dolorosa, whose memory has inspired me to strive higher than the hills and treetops of her hometown.

*A leaf marred by the elements
but still on the vine, speaks for
each of us bravely taking up a
designated space in the universe
with resolute will.*

Introduction

Stuff happens in our lives. Zany, spooky, poignant, tough. All of them stimulating and challenging. Eventually we move on from our experiences, hopefully wiser from what we've learned. The Latin, *experientia* means knowledge gained by repeated trials.

We need to be reminded of things that have transpired; to be guided and correspondingly equipped as we steer our way through life's passages. There are memories recalled, diaries kept, journals written, and stories told.

"I want to write, but more than that, I want to bring out all kinds of things that lie buried deep in my heart," wrote 13-year-old Anne Frank in her diary.

American novelist Jack London encourages us to preserve our thoughts. "Keep a notebook. Travel with it, eat with it, sleep with it. Slap into it every stray thought that flutters up your brain. Cheap paper is less perishable than gray matter. And lead pencil markings endure longer than memory.

Regret follows wonderful ideas
if courage is not in step.

Sailor Moon

"Fighting evil by moonlight." These impassioned words, deceptively sugar coated yet fervent boldly launch Sailor Moon's theme song. The lyrics are earnest and intense, just like the eponymous gamine's crime-fighting adventures that riveted the imagination of youngsters in the early 1990s. This popular anime television series spun off the manga – Japanese comic book, written by Naoko Takeuchi. It heralded the daring exploits of a young girl as she is magically transformed by her kind act of saving a cat from danger.

Luna, the rescued cat with a distinct crescent moon marking on its head bestows to the girl, Usagi Tsukino, a special brooch. The amulet gives her power to protect the earth from energy-stealing monsters sent by the malevolent Queen Beryl of the Dark Kingdom. Sailor Moon, the feisty superhero alter ego of Usagi, must also search for the lost princess of the Moon Kingdom and other Sailor Guardians to save the planet from destruction.

Arriving decades ago, Sailor Moon essentially became the nascent female hero of recent times, and her valiant crusades can be ascribed as blueprints for women's empowerment. Equal opportunity and germane causes have increasingly fueled worldwide female activism. We've long known about the glass ceiling, chronicled back in 1986 by the Wall Street Journal's Carol Hymowitz and Timothy Schellhardt. They wrote of the invisible barrier that held back women from attaining positions of greater responsibility in the corporate world. "Erratic and emotional" was how President Nixon then viewed women's general disposition. Once women showed their strengths and capabilities to attain equal footing with men, the specter of exploitation and harassment emerged, cloaked in villainous forms such as what Sailor Moon zealously opposed.

*The basic precept of humanity is
to serve, show compassion,
and look out for others.*

Sailor Moon's mantra for repelling dangerous forces also translates to girding ourselves and confronting apprehensions boldly. A determined stance will illumine one's path, however faint it may glow. I recall the time our daughter, Adrienne, resolved to pursue her Mandarin language studies further. Barely 19, she looked beyond the challenges of travelling alone for the first time and making it to Shanghai for a five-week language and Chinese culture course. I'm certain her experience has also provided valuable insights that will prove purposeful in her career.

A pertinent and similarly vexing situation emerges. Our planet reels from the onslaught of humankind's haphazard stewardship of the environment. Use of fossil fuels and indiscriminate farming methods have contributed to altered weather patterns, among other extreme climactic events. The Amazon rainforest, called the lungs of the world as it draws in carbon dioxide and releases oxygen continues to show its vulnerability to climate change.

Brazil's extraction-based economy that expands farming and cattle raising is seen as a major cause. Summer comes earlier to the Amazon jungle as heat increases from deforestation, affecting the waterways as well as the wind and rainfall. "The expensive hoax that is global warming" is how President Trump dismisses climate change. In Sailor Moon's time she had her hands full with callous energy plunderers.

Sailor Moon has transcended pop entertainment to become a young exemplar of women's strength, perseverance, and compassion. Her stories are metaphors for virtue that can compel broad change in our world today. Nothing will get in the way of this transformative process. Women of all ages who aspire for every conceivable venture bravely follow in Sailor Moon's path toward her radiantly symbolic goal of "winning love by daylight."

I know I am but summer to your heart,
And not the full four seasons of the year.
-Edna St. Vincent Millay

The Blind Poet

I am too scared to even drink water
It may fade my beloved's name on my heart.

-Zaheer Ahmad Zindani

Zaheer Ahmad Zindani lost his father in an American airstrike while the man tended the family's small farm in Gereshk, Afghanistan. Zaheer was seven years old. After the funeral, his mother and all siblings moved to Kandahar, 69 miles away. There, he met a distant relative, also 7. They grew close and mutual affection happened through the years, even when his family moved to another place. But the love that blossomed between them was doomed. The girl was from a rich family, and Zaheer was just a mechanic's apprentice. One day on a bus ride to visit relatives in Herat Province, a Taliban roadside bomb ripped the vehicle and blinded the boy. Without his sight, poor and illiterate, he turned to poetry. His siblings wrote the poems he dictated.

The girl for whom Zaheer intended some foreboding and poignant lines was eventually married off by her family. His thoughts proved prescient. And since then Zaheer has pondered whether love lost is better than not to have loved at all.

Based on a New York Times news article by Mujib Mashal, July 1, 2018

Transitions

Any passage one survives
Leaves traces however nebulous
Even when you choose to forget
No emptiness is ever certain.

Edvard Munch's anxiety
Inexorable on a cliff's edge
Presages a dismal end.
But gaping eyes see beyond;
Impressions that linger forever.

A bird's life passage from its cage
Reveals to me with a wing outstretched –
A sign of eternal freedom,
The inevitable conclusion that all must face.
The other wing tucked under –
Evince thoughts that endure
As indelible memories wistful and stirring.

Fenixx has gone.
October 25, 2017

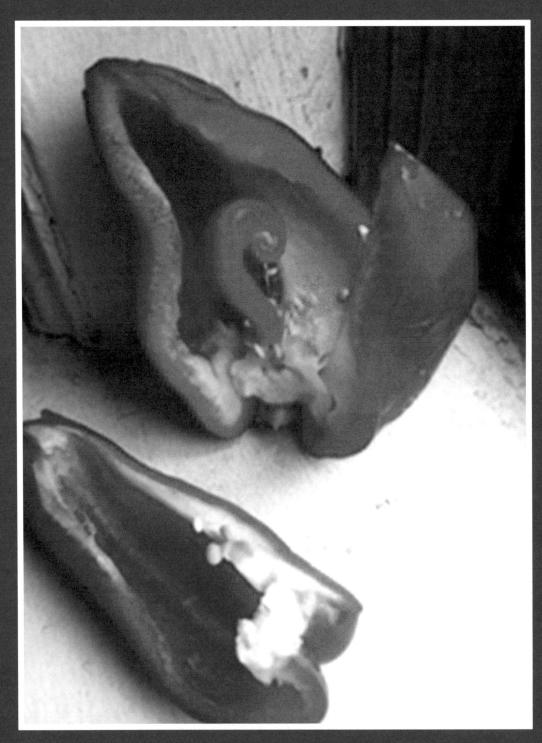

Mark Twain averred that like the moon, everyone
has a dark side, and they never show it to anybody.

Seeing Red

Red – the color of blood, has historically been associated with sacrifice, danger, and courage. Heat, passion, sexuality, anger, love, joy, and intense emotion are also commonly identified with this vivid hue.

During the Middle Ages, the Pope and Cardinals of the Roman Catholic Church used red in their vestments to symbolize the blood of Christ and Christian martyrs. In Chinese culture, good fortune and happiness are expressed in crimson, from the ubiquitous color at their New Year celebrations to the red envelopes that contain monetary gifts given during holidays and other special occasions. Red commemorates the union of two people in India; it is the preferred color of a bride's garment and the red spot (*tikka*) she wears on her forehead is a sign of her commitment. In this land of spices, red chilies are not only their most feisty ingredient but also connote the sensuousness and energy that is embodied in the ancient Indian Sanskrit text. Kamasutra focuses on sexual energy to express human creativity at all levels – physical, emotional, and spiritual.

The 16th century marked the serendipitous discovery of the red pigment by the Spanish conquistador Hernan Cortez. The explorer led an expedition to look for precious metals in Mesoamerica, and eventually caused the fall of the Aztec Empire in 1521. Gold was the treasure supposedly in abundance in the ancient American civilizations. But Cortez found an equally valuable commodity prized by European aristocrats at the time. He discovered the glowing carmine, which natives used to dye yarns spun from rabbit fur. To nobility, the color red exuded power and prestige.

A tiny red insect – the cochineal bug was dried and ground by Mayan artisans to produce the pigment. Cortez brought it back to Europe and was grown in Spain, Italy, North Africa, and other countries where the prickly pear cactus, favored habitat of the bug thrived. From the jungles of "Middle

Appreciate the people that give you joy.
Quietly they tend your garden
and all you see are bursting blooms.

America", a valued material essentially brought the regal color to Europe's palatial halls.

Red is also a sinister color. Let me tell you a story. During my teens, our home in Manila was a boarding place for quite a few relatives from the province who found a convenient city foothold for college. One cousin arrived after he had finished high school and a year at a Baptist seminary, then a dubious practice meant to prepare vulnerable youth against urban evils. In our home, my cousin slept on an old army cot in the hallway. My mother told me about the terrifying incident that happened to him one day.

The cousin was on his way home from school one night. My mother heard him whistling quite loudly as he walked in the dimly lit street toward our unlighted porch. She waited for his knock before opening the front door. Some minutes passed, then she heard what seemed like frantic scuffling. Quite alarmed, she turned on the porch light and opened the door. There passed out on the porch floor was my cousin. His books and papers were strewn around him. A gnarly branch was beside him. Long, fresh scratch marks ringed his neck.

His story unfolded minutes after he was revived by my agitated mother. On the bus ride home that night an eerily beautiful, pale looking woman had suddenly appeared and sat between him and another passenger. My cousin knew that only he could see her. Immediately the air in the bus turned chilly. The other passenger felt cold and closed the window beside him. The mysterious woman sat silently throughout the trip. My cousin added: she had two glistening ebony horns on her head and the color of the flowing gown she wore was a deep red.

It was not his first fearful encounter with the woman. There were other haunting incidents. One night while asleep in the seminary dormitory, my cousin startled his roommates as he began to levitate. Almost nightly at our home, he said the woman in red would rouse him as he slept on the cot. She would pester him to live with her in an otherworldly domain. She became annoyingly persistent, and her quest was about to end. That evening on the bus it was clear that her desperate attempts would be done more forcibly.

*Advice to the anxious mind: If you have
never done evil, you need not worry about
villains knocking at your door.*

She disappeared before my cousin reached his stop, sounding ominous about her later appearance. It alarmed him greatly to pick up a big stick, the only protection he could quickly think of as he walked the few blocks home.

The night's full moon hastily slipped behind dense clouds as his pace quickened. Trees by the road stood eerily still. Neighborhood dogs that turned raucous at any movement in the dark were unusually silent, even ignoring my cousin's shrill whistling.

Moments later the struggle on the porch ensued. Years of baleful cajoling and hushed nighttime visitations had ended. The woman's tempered pursuit was over. She had turned hostile. On our porch she lunged at my cousin with a fury, grabbing at him with vile force. The suddenness of the attack knocked him cold. On his neck were deep scratch marks from her fingernails. It was the first physical manifestation on his body of the evil clothed in red.

In the vastness of space we may be alone or
maybe not. If we try to determine alien superiority,
a clear sign of intelligent life is that none of it
has tried to contact us, deems Bill Witterson,
cartoonist and author of Calvin and Hobbes.

Life in Outer Space

Five-year-old Annika was on the phone with me. She was in Manila and I was in Philadelphia. This was sometime during the early 1980s. Over the crackling static of landlines in the nondigital era, my daughter asked, "Dad, is it nighttime over there?" I answered yes and wondered about her question. "Because I can hear the stars twinkling," she replied.

Through the years, outer space particularly extraterrestrials and UFOs have fascinated me. I pondered my daughter's whimsical remark and fancied: could there be more than turbulence in the earth's atmosphere that causes light from stars to be refracted and change brightness, and appear to be twinkling? Something out in the universe's vastness could be sending signals, trying to make contact with anyone farther from their realm. This is beyond sci-fi movies.

NExSS – the Nexus for Exoplanet System Science is the 2015 NASA initiative dedicated to the search for life on planets outside our solar system. The first exoplanet – a planet around another star like the sun was discovered in 1995 and more than a thousand others have since been found. Scientists are investigating for biosignatures, or signs of life on them. Meteorites may contain fossilized remains of some life forms or organic particles. Early in 2018 Italian researchers announced they had found evidence of a lake that existed on Mars, and water on its frigid landscape has been confirmed in the form of ice and hydrated minerals. Water is one of the universal ingredients required for life on Earth and its presence elsewhere holds much promise. Research points to the right direction and more definitive evidence about some form of life in outer space could be found within my lifetime, as NASA scientists predict.

Consider much earlier records of alien contact. The Mayan Dresden Codex was written between the 12th and 14th centuries by indigenous people of

*Imagine aliens present in our world today, but
keeping their distance and observing us in silence –
like watching a bacterial culture in a Petri dish,
waiting to see how long it avoids self-destruction.*

the Yucatan Peninsula in southeastern Mexico. It contained astrological tables and ritual and divination calendars, eclipses of the sun and moon, instructions to new-year ceremonies, and is said to mention linkups with extraterrestrials. Deep in the Mexican jungles are what seem to be landing pads claimed to have been left by visitors from the skies 3,000 years ago. Artifacts allegedly created by Ancient Maya were presented by Dr. Nassim Haramein at a conference in Germany in 2011, and seem to depict spacecraft and ancient astronauts.

The imaginable existence of technologically advanced beings in the cosmos continues to intrigue and goad humankind to seek for answers. Also, people can proffer far-fetched concepts unsupported by any evidence in order to uphold an idea. Sherlock Holmes proposed that when you have excluded the impossible, whatever remains, however improbable, must be the truth.

Phenomenal strides in science astound us, even as a Space Force is being proposed to become the sixth branch of the United States Armed Forces. Countless innovations have arisen, many tangentially in the quest for greater space exploration. It will be difficult for me to live without products of nanotechnology. I have eschewed landlines and my bulky DSLR camera for a palm-size cellphone with 12 awesome megapixels. My first digital camera had 2.5 megapixels. Artificial intelligence will soon enable circuit breakers to stop nuisance shut-offs of appliances when there is no discernible danger. I can keep on vacuuming and not have to worry about false risks posed by power fluctuations. 3-dimensional printing creates inexpensive artificial limbs for the disabled and an actual piece of sculpture straight from my sketchpad drawing. Even the speed of Amazon Prime boggles my mind. It is actually nothing but high-integrity parcel sortation solutions that involve innovative image capture and scanning technology. All I care about is fast and free delivery. And that's the compelling benefit for people like me with toned-down extraterrestrial interest.

It's a breakneck pace of developments happening in our planet that even reading the hefty Sunday paper takes me almost a week. There is so much to absorb and account for in our daily routines. I will allow the scientists to pursue beings that may be lurking in the firmament. I further opine that although life may extend way out in the stars, there still is greatness that figures in ordinary human's earthbound aspirations.

Fall Haiku

Autumn

Hold still and hearken
Outside it's winter's footsteps –
Sound of falling leaves.

Early November

Is the sun rising?
Mumbles a restless sleeper
A rooster responds.

Pensando

Words are effaced by
Sun and rain but thoughts linger
Interminably.

Graffiti transcends mere random squiggles
to impart the artists' raw, uncensored
messages with stylized images. On the walls
of Jersey City's pre-war buildings is the modern
version of the Lascaux cave paintings in France.

High Art, Low Art in NYC

An art theorist and critic once posited online that high art is appreciated by those with the most cultivated taste while low art – accessible and easily comprehended is for the masses. The implication that one art form is edifying and the other is simply entertaining arose from the 18th century distinction between fine art and craft. Why can't art manifest both attributes and be enjoyed by everyone without any preconditions?

On a chilly afternoon in February 2005, I experienced a stimulating art installation in New York's Central Park. *The Gates* by Bulgarian artist Christo Yavacheff and French artist Jeanne-Claude was set up along 23 miles of meandering pathways. Saffron-colored nylon fabric panels were hung over 7,503 rigid polyvinyl frames 16 feet high. From a rocky hill I observed the banners billowing in the late winter breeze like a languorous serpent.

The artist duo's project was conceived nearly 30 years earlier and was self-financed at a cost of 16 million dollars. Many art critics dismissed the installation, I presumed, after taking it as an affront to their button-down sensibility of purposeful art. Others objected to its intrusion on the city's prime nature landscape. *The Gates* represented a threshold, a portal that had no distinct area of entry or exit. There was no suggested vantage point to view a designated central focus; the structures were meant for people to walk through. It was expected that one came to it with no preconceived notions or expectations. As the sun slowly disappeared behind the skyscrapers, I sensed the incipience of spring in the extended assembly of flapping banners, radiating a message of hope in the bright color against a bleak backdrop. That was my own experience.

On a sidewalk in midtown Manhattan, a man sat surrounded by big boxes filled with empty soda cans. I watched intently as he easily cut off the tops of the empties with a pair of scissors. Then he used a box cutter to make

Artisanal handicraft – useful and decorative
objects made completely by untrained hands
with simple tools and creative minds.

vertical slices around the cans, which he deftly twisted and shaped into curly forms. What emerged were colorful and inventive tea candle holders. A crowd that had gathered were amazed at his seemingly untrained artistry.

Outsider art, a term coined by art critic Roger Cardinal in 1972 describes art created beyond the boundaries of the mainstream art world. It also referred to work done by people with mental incapacities. Unconventional ideas were explored and unusual materials were used for creations that could also serve utilitarian purposes. Grandma Moses was a self-taught American folk artist who started painting in earnest in her late 70s and gained worldwide renown for simple compositions of rural life.

The mysterious British street artist, Banksy, transformed his graffiti skills to become a visual commentator on social issues. In 2013 he put up a month-long installation/exhibit around New York City. His art cropped up in various locations with intriguing results. In one instance, he hired an elderly man to run a nondescript stall in Central Park to cheaply sell some of his original, signed canvasses. People did not catch on to the pop-up Banksy display, which figured like a direct riposte to accusations by critics that he was manipulating his notoriety for the skyrocketing prices that his work had generated.

My bold foray into New York's mainstream art scene started around the late 1980s. I made an audacious attempt to interest galleries in downtown Manhattan with my art. Combing the artsy area called SOHO, I eagerly attempted to present my watercolors. Unaware of the protocol that involved artists representatives and art dealers, I naively walked into the art shops with my humble portfolio. The response I got was perfunctory. My work was deemed mere illustrations, therefore could not merit display on galleries hallowed walls. So, I went directly to the masses and offered my art to pedestrians on the sidewalk. I recall a young boy, about 10 years old who expressed interest in one of my postcard size acrylics on paper. It was a representational scene of the bright sun blazing behind a bamboo tree. The price was fifteen dollars but the boy only had 7 dollars. He walked away crestfallen that he could not buy the small painting. Minutes later he came

*Art in NYC pops up anywhere and may look
outlandish but no one says, "You've gotta be
kidding." If you take a photo, the artists may
accost you for a donation. Starving artists
got to have a burger sometime.*

back to haggle for it. I did not hesitate to sell the painting for all he had in hand. His obvious joy was priceless.

Art is a commodity. But its value need not be pegged solely on intellectual postulations or assessed for monetary worth but on the experiential impact it generates.

Mark Bradford, 57, a former hair stylist is an American artist living in Los Angeles. His abstract work combines dense layers of brightly colored paper, paint, and rope. The gnarly, thought-provoking compositions have gained international acclaim and command astronomical sums.

He surely benefited from erudite evaluations of his art. An equally valid assessment came in a forthright critique of his work by a former hair salon customer. Bradford had gifted the woman with a painting in his signature style. She said, "I don't understand it but it's beautiful."

Dreams can come true.
Without that possibility,
nature would not incite us
to have them.
            -John Updike

Dreams

I had a perplexing dream once. I was in an auditorium, watching surreptitiously from behind a lush parlor palm as officemates in formal wear filed up a stage. They were going to present a concert. I was envious that I wasn't part of the group. In reality, I had been fired from my job. What else could the dream mean?

In 5,000 BC, Sumerians viewed their dreams as signs sent from the gods. The earliest recorded dream is from the Sumerian king Dumuzi of Uruk, who dreamt of an eagle that seized a lamb and a falcon that caught a sparrow. The king's sister offered an ominous interpretation that foretold his well-being, and for his safety advised to make himself scarce. Ancient Egyptians had a Dream Book of rituals and prayers to interpret dreams. Around 335 BC, Greek philosopher Aristotle declared that humans are capable of achieving pure form of wisdom only during sleep. Thus, dreams played a significant role in every aspect of their lives, from implementing military strategies on the battlefield or deciding on practical options to benefit families at home.

Hippocrates, regarded as the father of modern medicine, was first to realize that dreams were valuable indicators of physical and mental health. It was also contended by other learned men that dreams streamed from human thoughts and did not come from a divine source. Scholars then openly proclaimed that dreams were inspired by people's own proclivities, emotions, and experiences of everyday life and were not messages from gods.

It is not uncommon for dreams to stimulate creativity and provide direction for one's passions. Abstract expressionist Jasper Johns revealed that he once dreamed he had painted a large American flag. When he woke up he immediately set out gathering materials to start painting. He has become well known for his depictions of the American flag, a distinct motif in his work.

Many times, the dreams I have while awake
lapse seamlessly into the dreams when I'm
asleep. Especially, the prodigious ones.
So far, they've all come true.

Different cultures have developed their own traditions to interpret dreams. As far as I can recall, none of my dreams had any earth-shaking global implications or created demonstrable excitement on my humdrum life. There was news in recent years of four people who said that dreams about a combination of numbers resulted in huge lottery winnings for each of them. No such luck for me. But it is amusingly fanciful to consider what British psychologist and pioneer dream researcher Ann Faraday thoughtfully postulated. She proposed the "science of understanding our dreams [as] learning a language of our hearts." No algorithms involved.

Daughter, Why the Furrowed Brow on a Pristine Morning?

A blizzard swept over us last night.
Now a downy cloak stretches
From our feet to the blank sky.

The park seems to have been scrubbed clean.
For us it is a chance
To create graffiti footprints.

We stomp our boots and startle the pigeons
Huddled on the ground like patterns
Of a blotched and tattered quilt.

In a moment the ruffled flock disperses,
Then seeks out a fallen branch
Sticking sharply from the snow.

The early light is shaken briefly
By the pulse of beating wings
That rend the serene terrain.

Between extended pauses our muffled voices
Spill random thoughts; quickly forsaken
Like punctuations of frozen twigs on the landscape.

We behold the field restored to halcyon
By light snow falling as we turn and
Start for home in a warm handclasp.

*When you are young, it is difficult to keep
still. Like the year that becomes restless
to move on, and changes seasons.*

Incident at the Shed

I have no clue what the shed was for. A rusty corrugated steel structure, about 12-foot square, abandoned because it could have outlived any peculiar use. It may have been the elementary school janitor's office, until the windowless box became like an oven in Manila's tropical heat. Located on the far end across from our school building, it stood forlorn by the west wall of the property. A botanical garden overgrown with dying plants and a long dried up reflecting pool were behind it. There was no lock, even a simple latch to keep the rickety building shuttered. Not a visible trace of human activity could be detected; earthworms etched squiggly lines on its dusty cement floor.

Most of the school kids knew about the shed but were never curious to venture anywhere near it. There was nothing exciting about the place where it stood. No trees for shade against the hot sun or lend springy branches for the foolhardy graders to swing on. Only scraggly cogon grass grew high, hiding small brown grasshoppers that leaped crazily over each other. The tall brown reeds offered momentary rest for pin-thin damselflies. Quickly they zigzagged in tireless patterns then stopped abruptly on the stiletto blades. Sometimes a wayward gust would disperse the white fluffy tops of the spindly weeds. Nothing else moved. The shed was left alone as the kids quickly drifted home soon as classes ended.

But one stifling afternoon was different. Some boys in our fourth-grade class were not too eager to get home yet. Maybe about ten of us giddily ambled across the open field from the school building. No one talked as we cautiously made our way to the shed.

Earlier that morning in the playground I had verbally sparred with a classmate over something stupid. I forget how it started but the words that we lobbed harshly at each other just grew sharper and more ludicrous. During recess

Sunlight through the leaves casts shadows
that shift constantly. To see things clearly,
one should focus not only on what's in the light
but on the shapes formed by darkness.

we kept at it and by lunchtime, egged by unruly classmates, we had agreed to settle everything in a fistfight. In the shed, after school.

The other kid was the least likely adversary I could have picked. He was the most reticent guy in class and was the captain of our section's basketball team. He also stood a head and a half over me. But it did not matter, I was not backing down. My misplaced childhood honor was at stake. So off to the arena we went.

Inside the shed our classmates excitedly gathered in a circle around us; everyone was anxious to witness the brawl unfold and see who would emerge with less bruises. The tall kid with a ramrod stance warily eyed the short kid who bobbed nervously. And we raised our fists. There was no hesitant posing or cautious circling. We just flailed at each other like street dogs fighting over scraps; like mongrels ripping each other apart to settle a territorial dispute. I do not remember being fueled by such intense emotion. I only wished the senseless bout would end quickly. The better to get home before my mother wondered why I was a few minutes past my usual arrival.

The silly tussle was quick. It was a draw. The kid's nose was bloodied and I got an ugly shiner. Our classmates hollering had also drawn attention of the Junior Police – older kids tasked with enforcing rules of decorum in school. Both of us clumsy protagonists were hustled to the principal's office where each gave statements about what had transpired. Interviewed separately, I proffered a tearful account of the silly event, trying to elicit dubious pity.

My parents were summarily apprised of my transgression and I won't forget the swift and stinging discipline when I got home. Days after the incident I lost track of my former opponent. He might have transferred to another school. I stayed on and got into more placid endeavors. My homeroom teacher kept me after school to write paragraphs and nurture incipient literary skills that she sensed. I started to like drawing, mostly copying comics characters from the funny pages of newspapers. The structure of poetry began to engage me while I enjoyed the random manner of sketching. Memory of my rite of passage at the shed began to fade.

*In youth you may do as you please and for
the most part there is time to change theories.*

I wonder if the shed was ever bolted shut or eventually torn down. It brings to mind the desolate barn in Andrew Wyeth's painting, *Christina's World,* a remote place of mystery to me. What might be hidden in the old barn set on a hill, or are there any veiled suggestions? Just as one can only guess about the building's interior, even the expression on Christina's face is unseen.

One night as I awaited sleep, a thought came over me. The shed could also be like a secret compartment inside our head. A place where things are kept until we find the time to do whatever was needed with them – situations that had to be dealt forthwith but at the moment were deemed bothersome in the rush of our lives. A hurt that had festered and needed to be resolved, an apology waiting to be expressed, a deferred opportunity to make amends, words of gratitude or appreciation left hanging – it's all there filed in the shed of our brains, where competing thoughts swirl. Then suddenly, an unlikely trigger sets off the recall alarm.

Time flies like an arrow sent. You can't call
it back, you can't slow it down, you won't get
another chance to think about where
it's supposed to go.

Jersey Diary

Last fall, a friend and his son took turns on a nighttime drive from South Carolina to their home in New Jersey. To keep alert on the last few miles, they decided to stretch their legs and get take-out coffee at a turnpike rest stop. Stepping out of the restaurant, my friend decided to use his cell phone to call a relative back in South Carolina. He was unaware that two state troopers were standing within hearing range.

"We'll be home in a few minutes," my friend said on the phone. "Not to worry about Uncle George; he's been tucked snug in the car trunk the entire trip." Then he turned in the direction of the two figures who seemed to be eavesdropping on his call. Face to face with the wide-eyed officers, my friend suddenly realized their reason for concern.

Everyone shared a laugh as my friend revealed that Uncle George was indeed resting in a tightly sealed urn placed in the back of the car after cremation in South Carolina.

Reprinted from the New Jersey Section, *The New York Times*, February 25, 2001

If I do not know where I'm going, I'm never lost.

12 Zones

The New Jersey commuter train lazily shuffles from Newark Penn Station, southward to Trenton. A few minutes out, I stare down the elevated tracks from my left-side window seat and see some horses sleepily meandering in a cramped paddock. I am quite baffled. The cheek-by-jowl jumble of apartments, car repair garages, laundromats, Spanish restaurants, and a motley cluster of small shops can still squeeze horses in this sardine can mix. There seems to be elbow room for animals otherwise fit for a countryside barnyard. The horses couldn't be destined for the NJ Meadowlands racetrack, I guessed. Not with all the city fumes they suck in at all hours. The story behind this misplaced urban corral is still a mystery to me.

Nine train stops further is the Edison station. Near it appears a modest single-story building with a tall signboard by its gated entrance. The plexiglass panel has the familiar silhouette of a mighty stallion rearing on its hind legs. It is the Ferrari logo. At first, I thought the place was a scrap yard; discarded car parts and detritus are piled high in the property's overgrown backyard. It is actually the Central Jersey dealership of the Italian luxury sports car. As the train zips southward, I always enjoy a fleeting glimpse of shiny Quattroportes moved out from the car showroom to bask in the sun like pampered thoroughbreds. I checked on their website and found the cheapest vehicle on the lot, a 2012 pre-owned Ferrari California T. The silver, 2-door convertible with interior in full Nero leather – premium steer hide, was offered for the price of six 1995 Nissan Pathfinder SUVs, my own ride at that time.

Chugging thirty miles more and another 3 stops away, the train rumbles into the Hamilton station – the penultimate stop on my daily rail commute. There, I behold more open vistas than along other stops. Trees and grassy fields replace earlier scenery of office buildings, hospitals, colleges, and

*When the contents of a cup are of paramount
importance on an arduous journey, Lumiere
the coffee guy becomes vital to my long commute.*

bedroom communities. Prominently standing out on the station's west side is a solitary, low-slung building that was once the factory of the world's leading manufacturer of plumbing fixtures.

The American Standard Brands logotype is still emblazoned on what is now an office building - the American Metro Center, but bygone ambiance lingers on, sort of. Like a cheeky nod I would suggest, to the commode maker's century-old headquarters, an incinerator behind the building emits pungent emanations strong enough to rouse napping train riders.

Hamilton station's east side offers a more engaging vista—the idyllic 42-acre Grounds For Sculpture, founded in 1992 by artist and philanthropist John Seward Johnson II. He's famous for giant statues like that of Marilyn Monroe holding down her windblown skirt and *Unconditional Surrender*, which depicts a wartime nurse swept up in an ardent kiss by a U.S. sailor. An exact replica of the 26-foot tall Marilyn Monroe statue teases commuters from the sculpture grounds that abut the train tracks.

The Trenton Transit Center is the last stop on my train ride. This is how I made it happen every work day: I had to be out our front door at 5:30AM for a bus ride to Journal Square Plaza in Jersey City. There, I caught the 6:00AM Port Authority Transit-Hudson (PATH) train to get to the Newark Penn Station. Then I hopped on the 6:28AM train to Trenton, which arrived at its destination at 7:38AM. It took two more bus rides and a quarter mile walk to reach my office building. At 8:30AM I was finally seated in my cubicle.

At 3:00PM, I would do the same thing but in reverse to get home. Six hours a day, five days a week for 12 months totaled 1,440 hours that I spent on the road every year. Nasty rain or snow storms, power outages, cancelled trips or when a despondent soul jumped on the tracks (happened twice on my journeys) caused delays that tested my Zen composure no end. I figured my commute hours filled 60 days annually.Ten vacation days and about 6 official holidays a year offered gratifying respite for me. It exhausts me now just to recall my travel routine for almost eight years. Small consolation that in my final two years of employment I was allowed a couple days each week to work from home.

*Long shadows chase a harried commuter
eager to get home after work. Next day,
the pursuit begins in earnest when dawn
breaks and it's the job that calls.*

Before the killer commute, and for the first seven years of employment at the organization I worked for, my travel was uneventful. Home in Jersey City was a mere three miles away. I had a postcard perfect view of the Manhattan skyline across the Hudson River. Steps from the building was a riverfront promenade where free lunchtime concerts happened every summer. I could even pick up our daughter from her grade school a few minutes away. I'd have her occupied for a couple of hours at a vacant workstation in my office until we left for home. That was an ideal job set up for me while it lasted. Then our office succumbed to its spiraling lease.

NJ Transit's northeast train corridor line traverses 12 zones – set by the NJ Transit Authority, and is strung together by 17 stations. My 12-zone (maximum) monthly pass permitted unlimited train and bus rides on any day and to anywhere in New Jersey. The pass allowed a direct route three-quarters of the way to my destination; it also offered tempting options to humdrum workplace commute. There were times I wished to have called in sick and hopped on the coastline train for the beaches along the Jersey shore. Who wouldn't have done just that while musing on 68 miles of daily travel to work. Although far from the scale of Homer's Odyssey, my true-life experience is both onerous and amusing to recall. How did I find any solace in such daunting circumstance? To survive, you must tell stories, encouraged philosopher and novelist Umberto Eco. It is sage advice.

New York City, it's for sights as well as for shopping. You can do both down Fifth Avenue.

A Comic Odyssey Manila-Philadelphia-New York-New Jersey

How many 30-pound rocks are needed to build a DIY septic tank? Is pasta fattening? What libation is also referred to us "pop"? An endless stream of conundrums similar to these kept one Filipino's head spinning on being transplanted to American soil. I left Manila almost 18 years ago, limp from the slings and arrows of personal travails and burdened by as many emotionally soothing mementos as I could cram into a marmalade hued naugahyde suitcase.

Philadelphia was my first stop. What could have been more significant than making a fresh start in the City of Brotherly Love. Two younger siblings had set up stakes years earlier in this East Coast city made famous by Benjamin Franklin and Sylvester Stallone's "Rocky." In my brothers' cramped apartment I became their newest floor manager – claiming a portion of the living/dining room floor to spread my bedroll. It was the least discomfort I would experience in an unfamiliar place.

The first order of business after I had settled in was to find a job posthaste. But with a resume that showed no local experience, my dream of applying vaunted ad-writing skills was like grasping smoke. No big deal, my first job as handyman at a used car lot paid tax-free cash. Washing and waxing an assortment of sedans and pick-up trucks all day also gave me ample opportunities to ruminate over David Ogilvie's advertising concepts. I had thoughtfully kept a magazine clipping that featured the techniques of persuasion by the "Father of Advertising." It was like doing meditation while repairing a busted internal combustion engine.

Buskers abound in the city sidewalks and subways with their pulsing sounds that keep you alert and entertained before your bus or train arrives.

One day, a unique opportunity in practical civil engineering was opened to me by the car lot owner. I was instructed to build a septic tank. Back in Manila, my only attempt at any kind of construction was building a double occupancy chicken coop out of wood strips recycled from an old *papag,* a kind of flimsy bed frame. Wielding a hammer and saw was the only heavy lifting I ever did. The septic tank project seemed daunting but was no cause for alarm to a fast learner. A quick lesson in cement mixing from my boss got me going. The hard part was heaving 30-pounds or so of granite chunks over the low property wall. The rocks rolled down a steep embankment to a gully that abutted a busy railroad track. I poured some cement mixture to keep the rocks from dislodging. After hours of deadlifting rocks, I imagined my limbs had extended a little longer as I waved to the motormen of passing commuter trains. But at day's end my septic tank was doing quite a job filtering slush from drainage pipes. I surveyed my handiwork with a neophyte builder's pride, not to mention a nice tan streaked with blue and crimson bruises.

A month of hands-on activity at the used-car lot was a cakewalk compared to the harsh challenge offered at my second job. It seemed that my Madison Avenue dream was seeing the light as I began work for a start-up pasta factory. Wholesome Fresh Pasta was owned by a Chinese family that had left the repressive regime of their country formerly known as Burma. After helping set up an Asian grocery in Philadelphia's Chinatown, the family's eldest son decided to venture into fresh pasta production. To the rest of the family the idea couldn't even stand a chance against their spicy pickled radish. That was basically the drift of all their contentious deliberations.

On a daily basis, amid churning out business proposal letters and creating tempting recipes for plain pasta dishes culled from old culinary magazines, I endured a constant barrage of the Chin family's bickering. Mounting promotional expenses for the pasta business and my exorbitant $115.00 weekly pay were the staple hot topics. That much I could figure out from the volley of their Mandarin language diatribes that assaulted my hearing at all times. I finally quit less than a month into the job. One pasta trivia I learned: it's not the noodles itself but the heavy meat-laden sauces that

*We carry our experiences like beads around
the neck. Too much and they weigh us down.
Too few and you need to get out more often.
Keep the ones that will make your life stand
out without calling undue attention.*

one piles on a pasta dish that beget killer calories. Extra virgin olive oil on roasted red peppers or cauliflower is a healthier option.

A more decent wage happened at my next employment with a local restaurant chain in Philadelphia. Faking experience as a waiter, I fumbled along initially as a cashier and host, seating groups of boisterous college students, penny-pinching old ladies, and corporate types. Within a couple months, I worked my way up to become a full-fledged waiter. On my first evening shift, I was assigned to the most trying restaurant station – a dimly lit mezzanine section that was accessible only via a narrow winding staircase. Despite rookie jitters, I was blessed abundantly that night. My first customer rewarded me with a twenty-dollar tip for a bill that was less than half that amount. It was not a mistake, I'm totally sure. Andrew Jackson was set upright in a neatly creased V on the table and not obscurely tucked under the salt and pepper shakers. To this day I wonder if it was my superb service or the cheap house Burgundy the customer ordered that unleashed such magnanimous benevolence. The drink was no better than soda pop.

The restaurant stint lasted three-and-a-half years, providing a steady income and free dinners. Evening shifts enabled me to get into freelance writing and working on my art during the day. Some college students who also waited on tables became my figure models in exchange for doing their portraits.

It was a series of oils with benignly posed nude female figures that got me in a hot spot years later when I relocated to New York. I included the paintings at my first solo exhibit in 1989 at the Philippine Center in Manhattan. Three large canvasses deemed objectionable for exhibit due to the nudes were taken down the gallery walls before the show's opening. Guests were confronted by empty spaces where I had hung the paintings. Invoking Philippine sovereignty on the piece of NY real estate occupied by the Center, the officials asserted their obligation to enforce certain strictures regarding exhibit content. Weeks before the exhibit, I had presented to the Cultural Officer photos of the art I would be displaying. There was no objection.

By fortuitous coincidence it was also the time when Robert Mapplethorpe's photo exhibit of nude men was raising the ire of some Washington politicians.

*I meet faceless travelers everyday,
not knowing where they are going.
Might they also wonder where I'm
headed? Just musings of a bored
and weary wayfarer..*

They objected to the support given the "pornographic" exhibit by the National Endowment for the Arts. The ensuing art furor caused quite a stir. My exhibit looked like my turn to be similarly chastised. Responding to the Philippine Center's brouhaha over my show, *The New York Post* described the Center's action as "prudish." Thereafter, I did not get a single invitation to any Philippine Center activity as I had always been favored before my exhibit.

Spring of 1989 came and I got through an interview and writing test for an office job. I landed an entry-level copywriter position at a scientific publishing company in New York. On my first day at work, I sat beaming before an immense steel desk in my cubicle. I was like a master of the universe, all gung-ho to demonstrate superb writing skills. A few seconds later I turned into a tadpole stuck in mud, straining to create sales copy for a book on Cardiovascular Reactivity and Stress.

Another stressful moment at the job occurred when our Selectric typewriters were junked for computers. My only mechanical expertise beforehand involved a vintage Underwood. The functions of Alt/Ctrl/Del/Esc on a PC were clear to me as Esperanto. MS-DOS sounded like an autoimmune condition, twice over. In near panic, I furtively spied on much younger colleagues as they deftly performed basic keystrokes to cut, paste, and save their drafts. Not a few times was I on the verge of dehydration trying to retrieve inadvertently deleted files or when searching for drafts lost in the black hole of unsaved documents. Good thing my memory had more byte to quickly reconstruct mislaid work.

For eight years I stuck it out at this grunt writing job. It seemed as if I had weathered the rigors of a double masters program. Workload was not determined by a rational schedule as projects were liberally heaped on our gang of four harassed copywriters. Brochures, flyers, catalogs, cover letters, book jacket copy, posters, mailers, leaflets, postcards, space ads – we cranked them out like hot biscuits. We thought of ourselves as advertising stalwarts at the McDonald's of the book publishing industry. In this fast and furious pace, I outlasted a total of 10 younger copywriters and two copy chiefs.

Unexpected residents can
mar any landscape.
An interloper gets the eye
stare in New Jersey.

I threw in the towel at the publishing company in 1997. By then, my wife and I had wised up about paying New York State taxes and moved across the Hudson River to Jersey City. I found a copywriting job with the marketing team of a national professional organization. It was a whole new writing experience for me with less onerous deadlines – more time to come up for air and do unhurried rewrites. The impressive Manhattan skyline, looming proudly like in a glossy tourist postcard replaced my old office window view of mesmerizing bricks. Commuter adventures had veered from dodging traffic and daredevil bike couriers to taking leisurely riverside strolls during lunch break. Getting home earlier meant I also had more time chasing after Adrienne, our frisky four-year-old daughter and shooing pesky squirrels that dug up our window flower boxes. "Life is short, eat dessert first," a wag once said. It's a delightfully compelling suggestion that I took to heart, as I enjoyed none sweeter moments attending to our toddler; keeping pace with her as she excitedly grew up.

Abridged from *Fil-Am – The Filipino American Experience*

Alfred A. Yuson, Executive Editor, 1999

It was a temperate time, decades ago when the
Twin Towers stood calmly with Lady Liberty—
symbols for all who worked together in peace.

Twin Towers

The shrill, piercing wail of sirens followed by angry cannon blasts of booming air horns hewed a clear path through lower Manhattan's noontime traffic. It was like Moses parting the Red Sea. Firetrucks barreled down streets and hurriedly cleared away vehicles as police cars, ambulances, and other rescue trucks also raced toward 150 Greenwich Street and two 110-story-high buildings. The iconic twin towers of the World Trade Center had been attacked by terrorists. At 12:17PM on February 26, 1993 a truck bomb was remotely detonated in the underground garage of the North Tower.

My office on Prince Street, a mile north of the World Trade Center complex had a clear sight of the higher floors of the twin towers. From the sixth floor of our building, I had a wide view of the lower Manhattan skyline dominated by offices in the Financial District and the world renown skyscrapers. Within minutes the area was a huge tangle of frantic activity.

That eventful winter afternoon was slightly overcast, coming out grey from a snowstorm that had dumped a few inches of slushy snow a week earlier. Arctic air dropped the temperature near the freezing mark and I wanted to be home early. But the workday would stretch a bit longer than usual. There was grim news to absorb and the subway trains had stopped running.

No one at work had definitive information about the incident. Not many in New York owned the bulky Motorola mobile telephones to quickly relay inquisitive calls. Google search would not be on the horizon until 1998. The friends I reached via landline offered wild speculations. What caused the fiery scene downtown? I peered out a window to see plumes of dark smoke swirling from one of the towers. I thought about its occupants. Each day 50,000 workers and 200,00 visitors filled its 10 million square feet of space. I imagined the place in chaos, pandemonium breaking out as people scrambled to escape the calamity. Checking for unfolding events from my

Gone in an agonizing instant.
Time moves on in one direction
while memory goes the other way.

window view, I could make out figures appearing in the north tower's sky deck. They were like scurrying ants that had nowhere safe to go. These were office workers escaping to the rooftop, away from the heat and fumes.

Soon helicopters appeared over the gathering crowd. The lumbering machines hovered over them perilously in the strong wind gusts. After some tense moments, the helicopters gingerly settled down in turns to load their panicky passengers. I was transfixed by the sight. It was a scene straight out of an action movie, with the danger obviously felt by all involved – the peril of a severely damaged structure and helicopters risking being swept by high winds into the building's communication tower. The emergency air shuttle plodded in the arduous process as daylight faded fast. Even as darkness fell, the rescue continued nonstop. All I could see were flashing hazard lights and power beams of the helicopters.

The impact of the 1,336 lb urea nitrate-hydrogen gas explosive packed in a rental van created a hole 200 feet by 100 feet, several stories deep. It caused the PATH train station ceiling to collapse, and was intended to send the North Tower crashing into the South Tower. The attempt failed but nonetheless caused casualties and major destruction. Six people were killed and over a thousand were injured.

Six suspects were convicted of directly participating in the bombing. Each one was sentenced to 240 years in prison.

-0-

September 11, 2001 started as a gorgeous morning. Bright sunlight illumined the Manhattan skyline like it was all set up for a travel poster photo shoot. I had found work in an office by the Hudson River in Jersey City. As I always did before settling at my desk, I gazed out the wide panel glass windows of our office to marvel at my stunning view of New York City. The Big Apple looked polished and serene against a seamless blue sky.

But not for long. At 8:46AM an ominous plume of dark smoke trailed out the middle section of the North Tower of the World Trade Center. I thought that it was too early for a helicopter crash in New York. Such fatal incidents had occurred as tourists were whisked around for a aerial view of Manhattan island, to end up in the Hudson River.

A new icon rises in Manhattan.
One World Trade Center – soaring for
hope and peace in a challenging planet.

My officemates and I crowded the windows, trying to figure out what had happened. Someone turned on a transistor radio. Newscasts reported a Boeing 767 aircraft, American Airlines Flight 11 had crashed into the building. It was an attack by foreign hijackers.

While we stood transfixed at the hellish sight, another airplane came into view, identified as United Airlines Flight 175. We saw it fly past the building, then amid our howls of shock, veer sharply into the South Tower. It was 9:03AM. At the plane's impact, shards of glass from the building's façade rained down, glinting in the sunlight like large sheets of tinsel. Soon after, people could also be seen flinging themselves out, driven by the intense heat from burning jet fuel. "Jumpers" is the firemen's clinical description of the desperate victims. The girls in the office began to cry. It is a vivid memory that sticks to my brain to this day.

Bedlam had ensued in the streets outside our building. People poured from their offices and rushed to get as far as they could from the horrific scene. All I could think of was a post-apocalyptic nightmare happening. Throngs were fleeing in all directions, fearing that more deadly airplanes would soon be falling out of the skies.

Our department's director came in our room and told everyone to move away from the windows. He hustled us into a conference room to apprise us of the situation. We were advised to leave for home immediately. As we sat in shock and silence, one of the guys offered a brief prayer for our safety.

I got a call from my wife to pick up our daughter from her grade school, half a mile from my office. Adrienne was with me in our car within minutes. As I was driving home, I noticed people spilling into my way, all looking aghast toward New York City. I pulled over in time to witness the North Tower collapsing. It had burned for 102 minutes. The time was 10:28AM. It looked like a huge stack of toy blocks being toppled. A fiery ring descended slowly one level at a time consuming the building until it disappeared in a massive eruption of debris and dust. A giant cloud of white smoke gushed skyward above an eerie void. Earlier, the South Tower had collapsed at 9:59AM, after burning for 56 minutes. A third building, 7 World Trade Center with 42 floors collapsed at 5:21PM. A count of 2,977 people perished at the WTC Complex that day.

At sunset New York still blazes with life as before.

My daughter and I got home, still incredulous at what had transpired. But where was my wife? Sandy worked at an office in midtown Manhattan. We had talked briefly before all landlines and cell phones went dead. I could just picture bewildered New Yorkers who didn't know how to reach their families.

My wife was at her desk at around 9:30AM when an officemate told her about a news broadcast of a fire at the World Trade Center. She didn't pay much attention until other officemates began adding bits of grim information. Many of them gathered in a conference room to watch live television coverage of the fire. The situation was turning more dreadful as minutes passed; people were trying to leave the city quickly as they could. Before long, Sandy joined her co-employees to make their anxious trek home. Public transportation was at a standstill. Uber rides had not been thought of then. From her office on East 59th Street, she walked toward the Hudson River pier on West 42nd Street and hoped to get on a commuter ferry to Jersey City. Only the Circle Line Sightseeing boats were giving rides. But there was a wait. A queue two miles long snaked up and down the path leading to the dock entrance. It took almost four hours before Sandy could finally board a boat. At the downtown piers, private boat owners offered rides to people caked in dust from the conflagration that raged behind them.

Sandy's boat ride brought her safely to one of the Jersey City piers. It was almost 6:00PM. A Jersey City bus shuttled the beleaguered commuters to a parking lot nearby for their final destination. From there I picked up Sandy. Her exhausting day came to an end at 7:30PM.

1.8 tons of wreckage and debris took nine months to clean up. The lives of thousands – survivors as well as families and friends of the victims had been cruelly shattered. The consciousness of the entire nation will be mired in unbelief for some time at the thought that true peace would ever happen in our world. It is a dismal reassessment of the optimistic words once spoken by Minoru Yamasaki, architect of the World Trade Center: "WTC should, because of its importance, become a representation of man's belief in humanity, his need for individual dignity, his beliefs in the cooperation of men, and through cooperation, his ability to find greatness." If only for my children and succeeding generations, my hope for this outcome springs eternal.

Rigoberto, Mirrored

He could not even see his face
Because the village streams had run dry.
The plastic folds stuck together in his pocket;
Why did he need a wallet when even the dent
Of the last Quetzal coin it held had vanished,
There was no work for him to earn them.
His children were idle at home
No school to go to not even a book to read.
The coffee trees on the mountainside were bent
Drooping at its branches not from fruit
But wilting under the sun,
The only steady presence day after day.
Hope had long been gone
From the Guatemalan highlands.

The father and his son, Alex, only 14,
Soon trekked the arid miles northward
To find hope and send some back home.

I wish I had more than the bread and sardines
On our table for their journey,
But I have these words
That may reach the eyes of others
Just as Rigoberto's story in the Sunday paper
Had met my own and sparked a thought.
Might a reflection of his earnest quest
Be seen in the ways we help our neighbors.

Who's coming and who's going. When at a
crossroads in your life there are choices to
be made. You just can't get off the ride and
leave things to chance. Reckon your options
with a dash of bravery.

He's Not Meh

Mediocre or unremarkable, he isn't. And that's my totally biased opinion.

Catching up on my son's activities over the phone is always a fascinating event I look forward to. Home is 10,000 miles east, which makes these rare conversations a lively occasion for accounts of the latest discoveries by an inquisitive 10-year old.

At one time, his spiel was about a black spider with yellow-banded legs. The distinct coloration, he asserted, was not only to blend with nature's pigments – an artfully devious camouflage against its predators, but a kind of fashion statement. With about 35,000 named species of spiders worldwide, one has to stand out with its own version of Tommy Hilfiger nautical stripes. Surely the ladies would take note. More recently, I listened to his authoritative-sounding, albeit gruesome discourse on how dragonflies stay airborne.

An experiment that involved plucking off the forewing, then hindwing of the insect provided my son the conclusive facts to explain his theories on arthropod aerodynamics. In a nutshell, he posited that the absence of wings had everything to do with directionless flight or disastrous gliding. But of equal importance was its sleek, elongated body that was essentially a spear, giving the dragonfly greater thrust and velocity through the air. For contrast, imagine a boxy beetle flying.

Momentary visions of having sired a future scientist or avionics expert, however, were set back with an importunate request from my youngster. Not for scientific tomes. But could I please send him a Transformers Autobot and a cassette tape of the latest hits by Tears For Fears.

Ripe mango paired with sticky rice deftly wrapped in a blade of a coconut frond is a delectable Philippine dessert.

Food – Some Mysteries and Memories

The sweet taste of a golden ripe Manila mango tarrying like ambrosia on the tongue. The satisfied belch after a manly bowl of creamy bisque with chunks of New England lobster. From the tropics to the shores of Maine, I can recall the places where I enjoyed food that stuck to my palate as well as my medulla oblongata. The brain part that controls breathing and heartbeat.

Food can quicken the pulse, like the insanely hot Sri Lankan dish called Kukul Mas curry, which made its way from ancient villages in Asia to the New World. Caravans traveled down the spice trade route through Asia, Northeast Africa, and Europe sometime around 1500 BC and transported an array of spices. Cardamom, cinnamon, cassia, ginger, pepper, nutmeg, cloves, saffron, and turmeric added distinct spicy flavors to meat and vegetable dishes of different regions along the route. They were among the most expensive and sought-after products between the 9 – 15th centuries, also used in medicines, perfume, wine, even for embalming the dead.

Spicy food helped cool down the itinerant traders on their journeys. Eating spices causes the body to sweat and once the moisture evaporates the body is cooled off.

Arabic spice merchants would create a sense of mystery about their wares by withholding its origins to ensure high prices. They told fantastic tales of fighting off winged creatures to reach spices growing high on cliff walls in lands unseen and unheard of.

Ancient lore added exotic allure to various foods. A mango's sweetness alludes to the compassionate conclusion of an old legend. There is a story of how

*Cheery colors belie the heat of fiery peppers
and chilies. Green is usually the hotter
chili than the red ones.*

a magpie flew to heaven and brought a mango seed back to its king. Once the seed grew into a tree and bore fruit, the king ordered an old man to eat the first fruit to determine if it was poisonous. It happened that the single piece of fruit had been poisoned by a snake's venom that had dripped onto the tree. The old man died and the horrified king killed the magpie. Much later, an old woman who had lived a miserable life with her abusive spouse came upon the tree. Penniless and hungry, she ate a mango from the same tree but was not poisoned. Instead, she gained back her youth; her reward for having endured a lifetime of suffering.

The lobster has strange anatomy. It hears with its legs and tastes with its feet. The kidneys are in the head, the nervous system in the stomach with its teeth, and its brain is in the throat. Once plentiful and poorly regarded as a food source in the 1600s, lobsters were mainly used as fertilizer by farmers. Not anymore.

Our daughter was four years old when we went on a family vacation to Maine, where the best lobsters are caught. At home, Adrienne would spend hours in her small inflatable pool in our backyard until her lips began to turn purple. At Ogunquit Beach on Maine's southern coast, it was no different as she splashed for hours in the cold Atlantic waters. Afternoons stretched beyond sunset as our daughter played in the shallows not minding the chilly air and water. Whenever I have a lobster dish, in a soup or plainly grilled I think of Adrienne enjoying the seashore until the stars started to show. With the constellations appearing, it was my Little Prince moment.

Food memories involve very basic, nonverbal areas of the brain that can bypass our conscious awareness, noted Susan Krause Whitbourne, Professor Emerita of Psychology at the University of Massachusetts, Amherst. That is why you can have strong emotional reactions when you eat a food that arouses those deep unconscious memories. You can't put those memories into words, but you know there is 'something' that the food triggers deep within your past. The memory goes beyond the food itself to the associations you have to that long-ago memory, whether with a place or person, explains Whitbourne.

*Maine lobster's succulent taste, a sweeter
version of crab meat without the fishy smell and
more meaty than shrimp could be the outcome of
genetics engendered by its topsy-turvy anatomy.
It's my unscientific explanation.*

Because food memories form without any conscious editing, they take on all attributes of the situations in which they were acquired. One's recollection of family meals gains additional emotional meaning that they become associated with certain smells and tastes.

French writer Marcel Proust, in his novel In Search of Lost Time recounted how eating a Madeleine cake as an adult instantly evoked memories from his childhood of seeing his aunt dip her Madeleine cake in tea. Such involuntary memory that elicits some past event has been known as a "Proustian moment."

My mother, Dolorosa baked the most delicious pineapple upside-down cake I've ever tasted. Moist and savory, its syrupy aroma – from the caramelized sugar and topping of lightly browned pineapple slices wafted all over our home as it baked in the oven. My eyes mist as I write about it now, and I begin to miss my mother.

So, on a few occasions I've asked my wife, Sandy to recreate the baking magic my mother did with basic ingredients and a simple recipe.

Simple and satisfying recipes bring warm
memories of my mother's home cooking.

Recipe for Old Fashioned Pineapple Upside-Down Cake

This recipe is a combination of a couple of recipes Sandy has tried for the perfect Pineapple Upside-Down Cake baked from scratch.

Ingredients

6-7 slices pineapple, canned or fresh – sliced to 3/8 inch each
¾ cup light brown sugar
1/3 cup butter
6-7 Maraschino cherries

Directions
Prepare pound cake batter and set aside.
Melt butter in a 9" square or round pan. Add light brown sugar, spreading it evenly on bottom of pan.

Arrange pineapple rings on the butter-sugar mixture. Place a cherry in the middle of each ring. Pour the cake batter (prepared ahead) over the pineapple arrangement.

Bake at 350 degrees F for 50-55 minutes or until a cake tester or a toothpick inserted in the center comes out clean.

Allow the cake to cool in the pan for 10-15 minutes, then loosen the sides and invert gently onto a cake plate.

Preparation time: 20-25 minutes
Serves 8-10

A childhood treat, pineapple upside-down cake wafts an aroma that is mother's silent call for kids to come home from play quickly.

Recipe for Pound Cake batter

Ingredients
2 cups cake flour
½ tsp salt
1 tsp baking powder
½ lb or 1 stick butter, softened
1 ½ cups granulated sugar
4 large eggs
½ cup milk, room temperature
1 tsp pure vanilla extract

Batter directions

In a medium bowl, sift flour before measuring. Measure and sift again with salt and baking powder, set aside.

In a mixing bowl, beat butter until light in color. Add sugar gradually and continue beating until light and fluffy. Add eggs one at a time, beating well after each addition.

Combine milk and vanilla in a measuring cup, set aside.
At this point, and using only a spatula, add flour mixture to the creamed butter alternately with milk, adding flour first and the last. Stir mixture until well blended.

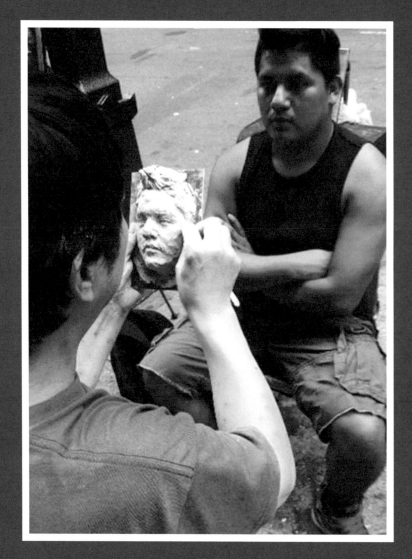

*Your portrait in 3-D while you
pose on a New York sidewalk.*

Everyone is entitled to take five
on a steamy day in Central Park.

*Things of art and beauty
are joys forever.*

Pondering the first move at
Exchange Place, Jersey City.